ULTIMATE
CAPTAIN AMERICA

ULTIMATE CAPTAIN AMERICA

WRITER:
JASON AARON

ARTIST:
RON GARNEY

COLORIST: **JASON KEITH**
WITH **JIM CHARALAMPIDIS** & **MATT MILLA**
LETTERER: **VC'S CLAYTON COWLES**
COVER ART: **RON GARNEY** & **JASON KEITH**
ASSISTANT EDITOR: **SANA AMANAT**
EDITOR: **MARK PANICCIA**

CAPTAIN AMERICA CREATED BY **JOE SIMON** & **JACK KIRBY**

COLLECTION EDITOR: **JENNIFER GRÜNWALD**
EDITORIAL ASSISTANTS: **JAMES EMMETT** & **JOE HOCHSTEIN**
ASSISTANT EDITORS: **ALEX STARBUCK** & **NELSON RIBEIRO**
EDITOR, SPECIAL PROJECTS: **MARK D. BEAZLEY**
SENIOR EDITOR, SPECIAL PROJECTS: **JEFF YOUNGQUIST**
SENIOR VICE PRESIDENT OF SALES: **DAVID GABRIEL**
SVP OF BRAND PLANNING & COMMUNICATIONS: **MICHAEL PASCIULLO**

EDITOR IN CHIEF: **AXEL ALONSO**   CHIEF CREATIVE OFFICER: **JOE QUESADA**
PUBLISHER: **DAN BUCKLEY**   EXECUTIVE PRODUCER: **ALAN FINE**

ULTIMATE COMICS CAPTAIN AMERICA. Contains material originally published in magazine form as ULTIMATE COMICS CAPTAIN AMERICA #1-4 and CAPTAIN AMERICA SPOTLIGHT. First printing 2011. ISBN# 978-0-7851-5195-1. Published by MARVEL WORLDWIDE, INC., a subsidiary of MARVEL ENTERTAINMENT, LLC. OFFICE OF PUBLICATION: 135 West 50th Street, New York, NY 10020. Copyright © 2011 Marvel Characters, Inc. All rights reserved. $14.99 per copy in the U.S. and $16.99 in Canada (GST #R127032852); Canadian Agreement #40668537. All characters featured in this issue and the distinctive names and likenesses thereof, and all related indicia are trademarks of Marvel Characters, Inc. No similarity between any of the names, characters, persons, and/or institutions in this magazine with those of any living or dead person or institution is intended, and any such similarity which may exist is purely coincidental. **Printed in the U.S.A.** ALAN FINE, EVP - Office of the President, Marvel Worldwide, Inc. and EVP & CMO Marvel Characters B.V.; DAN BUCKLEY, Publisher & President - Print, Animation & Digital Divisions; JOE QUESADA, Chief Creative Officer; DAVID BOGART, SVP of Business Affairs & Talent Management; TOM BREVOORT, SVP of Publishing; C.B. CEBULSKI, SVP of Creator & Content Development; DAVID GABRIEL, SVP of Publishing Sales & Circulation; MICHAEL PASCIULLO, SVP of Brand Planning & Communications; JIM O'KEEFE, VP of Operations & Logistics; DAN CARR, Executive Director of Publishing Technology; SUSAN CRESPI, Editorial Operations Manager; ALEX MORALES, Publishing Operations Manager; STAN LEE, Chairman Emeritus. For information regarding advertising in Marvel Comics or on Marvel.com, please contact John Dokes, SVP Integrated Sales and Marketing, at jdokes@marvel.com. For Marvel subscription inquiries, please call 800-217-9158. **Manufactured between 10/19/2011 and 11/7/2011 by R.R. DONNELLEY, INC., SALEM, VA, USA.**

10 9 8 7 6 5 4 3 2 1

PREVIOUSLY

America's first Super-Soldier, Steve Rogers,
became a living legend in the trenches of
World War II before being frozen for more
than fifty years beneath the Atlantic Ocean.

Now, after being found by Tony Stark, Steve
Rogers continues his fight to defend his country
along with the New Ultimates. In this, or any
other time, Steve Rogers is Captain America.

YOU'RE PRAYING? REALLY? YOU HONESTLY THINK GOD IS GOING TO WHAT, COME DOWN HERE AND SAVE YOU?

AFTER EVERYTHING I'VE SHOWN YOU, YOU STILL CLING TO YOUR PATHETIC LITTLE FANTASIES? THIS IS PATHETIC.

KISS.

MY.

ASS.

OKAY, YOU KNOW WHAT? ONE LAST LESSON, WE'LL JUST WAIT AND SEE. HOW ABOUT THAT?

WE'LL GIVE YOUR GOD, LET'S SAY, FIVE MINUTES. THAT OUGHTA BE PLENTY OF TIME FOR HIM TO COME DOWN HERE AND RESCUE YOUR ASS, RIGHT?

YOU JUST SIT RIGHT THERE AND KEEP PRAYING, CAP. I'LL GO WAIT OUTSIDE.

IN FIVE MINUTES WHEN I COME BACK IN HERE AND YOU'RE STILL KNEELING THERE, BABBLING LIKE AN IDIOT, I'M GOING TO WALK OVER AND PUT A BULLET IN YOUR BRAIN.

AND THEN YOU'LL DIE KNOWING EVERYTHING YOU EVER BELIEVED IN WAS A LIE.

KLANG-A-
KLANG-A-
KLANG-A

WHAT IN THE NAME OF...

WE'VE BEEN BREACHED!

WHO IN THE HELL ARE THEY?

JUDGING BY THEIR GUNS, I'D SAY BRITISH S.A.S.

THIS IS AN ACT OF WAR! GET THE DEFENSE COMMISSION ON THE LINE!

I CAN'T GET A LINE OUT! THEY'RE BLOCKING OUR COMMUNICATIONS!

OH GOD, THEY'RE GONNA KILL US ALL.

HEY, BIG GUY...C'MERE A SECOND.

WHAT DOES HE THINK HE IS DOING?

FRANK SIMPSON.

WHO THE HELL'S FRANK SIMPSON?

ONCE UPON A TIME, A GUY A LOT LIKE YOU. A KID RAISED ON APPLE PIE WHO LOVED HIS COUNTRY AND WANTED TO DO HIS PART.

"IN THE YEARS AFTER YOU DISAPPEARED, THE GOVERNMENT KEPT LOOKING FOR SOMEONE TO TAKE YOUR PLACE.

"FRANK SIMPSON ANSWERED THAT CALL."

YOU MEAN PROJECT REBIRTH. THEY GAVE HIM THE SAME INJECTIONS THEY GAVE ME?

NOT EXACTLY.

WITH YOU GONE AND DR. ERSKINE DEAD, REBIRTH HAD TO START OVER FROM SCRATCH. IT TOOK YEARS OF FAILURE BEFORE THEY DEVELOPED A SERUM THAT SHOWED ANY SORT OF PROMISE.

"SIMPSON WAS THEIR GREATEST SUCCESS.

"BUT EVEN THEN, THEY COULDN'T FULLY REPLICATE THE RESULTS THEY'D SEEN IN YOU. THEY HAD TO AUGMENT WITH CYBERNETIC IMPLANTS AND STEROID SUPPLEMENTS. ONE PAINFUL PROCEDURE AFTER ANOTHER.

"THEY PUT THAT POOR KID THROUGH HELL.

"IT'S NO WONDER HE EVENTUALLY SNAPPED."

THEY NEVER SHOULD'VE PUT HIM INTO COMBAT. HE WASN'T READY, BUT WE WERE FIGHTING A WAR THAT WASN'T GOING SO GREAT. NOBODY AT THE PENTAGON LIKED THAT MUCH. SO...

VIETNAM, YOU'RE TALKING ABOUT VIETNAM.

"POOR KID SIGNED UP THINKING HE WAS GONNA BE STEVE ROGERS STORMING THE BEACH AT NORMANDY, MACHINE GUNNING NAZIS. INSTEAD HE FOUND HIMSELF IN PLACES LIKE DAK TO, KHE SANH AND THE A SHAU VALLEY.

"THEY DUMPED HIM INTO A MEAT GRINDER AND LEFT HIM THERE.

"FOR FIVE YEARS.

"HIS KILL NUMBERS WERE STAGGERING. THE BRASS LOVED IT.

"THEY IGNORED THE TROUBLING SIGNS IN HIS PSYCH REPORTS. HELL, THEY DIDN'T EVEN BLINK WHEN HE GOT HIS DAMN FACE TATTOOED. THEY FIGURED THEIR NEW CAPTAIN AMERICA WAS GONNA TURN THE TIDE OF WAR.

"BUT THEN...

"THEN ONE DAY IN 1972, HE JUST WALKED INTO THE JUNGLE AND WAS GONE."

QUIT? JUST LIKE THAT?

MAYBE, BUT THERE WERE RUMORED SIGHTINGS MONTHS LATER THAT SUGGESTED HE HADN'T QUIT AT ALL.

JUST SWITCHED SIDES.

A $#@%& TRAITOR.

THEY TRIED TO BRING HIM IN. THEY SEARCHED ALL OVER, BUT THEN THE WAR ENDED AND HE WAS NEVER SEEN AGAIN, NOT FOR DECADES.

NOT UNTIL TWO DAYS AGO, WHEN HE KICKED YOUR ASS ON A ROOFTOP IN NORTH KOREA.

SO NOW HE'S WORKING FOR THE NORTH KOREANS TO DEVELOP A NEW SERUM.

THE DEAD SUPER-SOLDIER WE FOUND THERE, THE ONE SIMPSON TRIED TO INCINERATE. THE SERUM IN HIS VEINS IS A STRAIN DEVELOPED FROM SIMPSON'S OWN BLOOD.

OUR GUESS, HE'S BEEN SQUIRRELED AWAY SOMEWHERE FOR THE PAST SEVERAL YEARS, TRYING TO REVERSE-ENGINEER A SERUM. NOW HE HAS. AND HE'S SELLING IT. TO ALL THE USUAL SUSPECTS.

WE'VE HAD REPORTS COMING IN FOR MONTHS NOW OF SUPER-SOLDIER PROLIFERATION. IRAN HAS A PROGRAM IN THE WORKS, SAME WITH CHINA. AL QAEDA MAY EVEN HAVE ACCESS TO THE SERUM.

JUST TELL ME WHEN I'M GETTING OUT OF HERE AND GOING AFTER HIM.

YOU GET OUT OF HERE AS SOON AS THE DOCS CLEAR YOU TO RETURN TO DUTY. BUT AS FOR GOING AFTER SIMPSON, YOU CAN FORGET IT.

WE JUST NARROWLY AVOIDED ONE INTERNATIONAL INCIDENT. I'M NOT ABOUT TO BE ON THE BOOKS FOR ANOTHER.

I'M TURNING THIS OVER TO FURY'S BLACK OPS CREW. YOU'RE NOT TO GO ANYWHERE NEAR THIS MESS, DO YOU UNDERSTAND ME?

YOU WILL STAY HERE IN LOVELY, SCENIC FRANCE. I HEAR THE SNAILS ARE QUITE SCRUMPTIOUS THIS TIME OF YEAR.

CAMBODIA.

BEEN HERE MORE THAN A WEEK.

STILL LEARNING HOW TO BLEND IN.

UGH...

NO THANKS.

GOT ANYTHING THAT DOESN'T SMELL LIKE A CESSPOOL?

CAMBODIA WAS OFFICIALLY THE LAST PLACE SIMPSON WAS EVER SEEN. SO HERE I AM, TRYING TO PICK UP A TRAIL THAT'S DECADES OLD.

BEEN ASKING QUESTIONS AND GETTING NO ANSWERS. PLAYING DETECTIVE JUST ISN'T MY STRONG SUIT.

WAS ABOUT TO GIVE UP AND HEAD ELSEWHERE...

WHEN I REALIZED I WAS BEING FOLLOWED.

CONTACT HAS BEEN MADE. IDENTITY CONFIRMED. REPEAT, IDENTITY--

AAH!

NO!

COME UP AND CHAT WITH ME, PAL. GOT FEW QUESTIONS FOR YOU.

WELL, THAT ANSWERS MY FIRST QUESTION. YOU'RE NO SUPER-SOLDIER.

WHO SENT YOU AND YOUR FRIENDS HERE? WAS IT SIMPSON? FRANK SIMPSON?

SALOTH.

SALOTH? YOU'RE FROM SALOTH?

SALOTH, YES. HEH.

WHERE IS IT? TELL ME HOW TO GET THERE.

JUST KEEP GOING, SALOTH WILL FIND YOU, HEH HEH HEH.

THANKS.

AAAARRRGGHHH!

AAAARRRGGHHH!

IT'S ALL RIGHT, MA'AM. IT'S ONLY A FLESH WOUND. IT'S GONNA BE OKAY.

I PROMISE.

DOCTOR! WE NEED A DOCTOR HERE!

DOES ANYBODY SPEAK AMERICAN?

SALOTH. I'D HEARD THE NAME BEFORE.

A VILLAGE THAT DIDN'T APPEAR ON ANY MAP.

A CAB DRIVER IN SIEM REAP TOLD ME IF I WAS LOOKING FOR SOLDIERS, I WOULD FIND THEM THERE.

A BLIND BEGGAR ON THE STREETS OF PHNOM PENH TOLD ME IF I REALLY WANTED TO DIE, I SHOULD GO TO SALOTH AND THE SOLDIERS THERE WOULD BE HAPPY TO OBLIGE ME.

GUESS WE'LL SEE ABOUT THAT.

LOOKING AROUND AT THIS GODFORSAKEN PLACE, I COULD ALMOST UNDERSTAND IF SIMPSON HAD JUST SNAPPED.

I SAW THAT PLENTY DURING THE WAR. GOOD MEN WHO JUST REACHED THEIR BREAKING POINT.

SALOTH. GOTTA BE IT.

NO ABLE-BODIED MALES IN SIGHT, THOUGH. NOTHING THAT EVEN LOOKS LIKE A SOLDIER. JUST WOMEN AND CHILDREN AND THE ELDERLY.

SOME SUPER-SOLDIERS YOU GOT YOURSELF, SIMPSON. HIDING BEHIND THEIR GRANDMAS AND LITTLE SISTERS.

I COULD JUST HANG BACK NOW, KEEP AN EYE ON THE PLACE, SEE WHAT TURNS UP...

OR I COULD JUST WALK RIGHT IN AND START THROWING MY WEIGHT AROUND, SCREAMING AT PEOPLE.

IN MY EXPERIENCE, WHEN IN DOUBT...

DON'T BE AFRAID TO BE OBNOXIOUS.

FRANK SIMPSON! WHERE IS HE?! DON'T EVEN PRETEND LIKE YOU PEOPLE DON'T KNOW!

I CAN HELP YOU! I CAN GET YOU OUT OF THIS PLACE! JUST SPEAK UP AND TELL ME--

I KNOW WHAT YOU ARE LOOKING FOR.

WHAT THE HELL...

IT'S NOT YOUR FAULT YOU'RE SO NAÏVE, ROGERS. YOU WERE TRAPPED IN THAT ICE FOR A VERY LONG TIME.

LET'S BEGIN TO CATCH YOU UP ON SOME OF WHAT YOU MISSED, SHALL WE?

TODAY'S LESSON... *RICHARD MILHOUS NIXON*...

THE MOST EVIL MAN WHO EVER LIVED.

TODAY WAS A GOOD START.

GET YOUR REST NOW AND THINK ABOUT WHAT YOU LEARNED.

SLAM!

THE NEXT DAY...

RISE AND SHINE, TIME FOR ANOTHER--

GHK!

RRAAH

STAND DOWN. I DON'T WANT TO HURT YOU.

DO NOT WORRY.

YOU WON'T.

I'VE BEEN MORE THAN PATIENT WITH YOU, CAPTAIN. I'VE TRIED TO HELP YOU COME AROUND, BUT YOU INSIST ON STAYING BLIND, DON'T YOU? WELL NOW...

GRRRRGGHH!

NOW YOU'LL *HAVE* TO SEE.

YOU'RE A *KILLER,* AREN'T YOU? YOU'RE AN ASSASSIN.

NO, I'M A...I'M JUST A SOLDIER.

YOU WERE SENT HERE TO *SLAUGHTER.* TO KILL US ALL. TELL ME THE TRUTH.

TELL ME!

YOU'RE AN ASSASSIN! YOU'RE A KILLER, ADMIT IT!

AAARRGGHH!

AAAAAAHHH!

ADMIT IT!

YES...

YES!

BUCKY?

DO YOU KNOW...THE ONE THEY CALL...THE *JUSTIN BIEBER*?

HENG!

GET BACK TO YOUR POST.

RRAAAH

YOU ARE NOTHING IF NOT PERSISTENT, ROGERS, I WILL GIVE YOU THAT. BUT MY PATIENCE HAS FINALLY RUN OUT. I'M SORRY I COULDN'T HELP YOU, I TRULY AM.

GOODBYE, CAPTAIN AMERICA. IT'S BEEN A PLEASURE.

GO TO HELL.

ARE YOU... PRAYING?

IN FIVE MINUTES, WHEN I COME BACK IN HERE AND YOU'RE STILL KNEELING THERE, BABBLING LIKE AN IDIOT, I'M GOING TO WALK OVER AND PUT A BULLET IN YOUR BRAIN.

AND THEN YOU'LL DIE KNOWING EVERYTHING YOU EVER BELIEVED IN WAS A LIE.

I'M NOT GONNA BEG. NOT ANYONE.

NOT EVEN YOU.

I WILL FIGHT THIS MAN WITH EVERY LAST OUNCE OF LIFE IN MY BODY. I WILL DIE IF I HAVE TO.

I JUST WANNA KNOW THAT THERE WAS A PURPOSE TO IT, TO ALL OF IT.

I JUST WANNA KNOW.

GAAA...YOU *PIG-HEADED* SON OF A BITCH...

YOU COULD'VE HAD AN *EASY* DEATH. COULD'VE LEFT SOMETHING BEHIND FOR THEM TO BURY IN *ARLINGTON.*

BUT NOW I'M GONNA FEED YOU TO MY *PIGS,* ONE PATHETIC LITTLE SCRAP AT A TIME.

C'MON!

AFTER I BASH YOUR BRAINS IN, ROGERS, I'M GONNA HANG YOU UP AND BLEED YOU OUT LIKE A DEER.

AND THAT *BLOOD* WILL FEED THE CAUSE FOR YEARS TO COME.

YOU'VE GOTTEN ENOUGH BLOOD OUTTA ME ALREADY, SIMPSON.

BUT I'LL TAKE A BIT MORE OF *YOURS*.

GUHH

AHH

ADMIT YOU WERE WRONG, ROGERS. OR I PROMISE YOU, THIS WILL GO ON FOR *HOURS.*

ADMIT YOU'RE THE TOOL OF AN IMPERIALIST REGIME. THAT ALL YOU KNOW ARE *LIES* AND PROPAGANDA.

THAT AMERICA IS DEAD. AND *YOU* HELPED KILL IT.

ADMIT YOU WERE WRONG, ROGERS! WHILE YOU STILL HAVE TIME! ADMIT IT!

OKAY...

OKAY, I ADMIT IT. I WAS WRONG, ABOUT ONE THING AT LEAST.

NNNNNNNGGGHHHH!

YOU GOT SOME STONES AFTER ALL.

YOUR DAY IS COMING. THE DAY YOU'LL LOOK BACK AND REGRET NOT LISTENING TO ME, AND CURSE YOURSELF FOR BEING SUCH A FOOL, THE DAY YOU'LL FINALLY REALIZE...

YOU'LL SEE.

YOU'VE BEEN *LIED* TO ALL ALONG.

I JUST WISH I COULD BE THERE TO SEE IT. HEH HEH HEH.

CAPTAIN ROGERS.

YES, SIR.

OPEN IT.

WHAT DO YOU WANT, ROGERS? COME TO GLOAT?

NOPE.

JUST RETURNING A FAVOR.

HOLY BIBLE

GOING TO WAR WITH ULTIMATE CAPTAIN AMERICA!

WRITER JASON AARON TAKES UP ARMS WITH A DECIDEDLY DIFFERENT STEVE ROGERS

BY JESS HARROLD

COVER TO *ULTIMATE CAPTAIN AMERICA* #2 BY RON GARNEY.

Like your Captain America with a little more edge? A Sentinel of Liberty who'll do anything — and everything — to get the job done? Jack Bauer with an "A" on his head? Then Ultimate Cap is the man for you. The Super-Soldier star of *The Ultimates* and *Ultimate Avengers* finally has his own limited series in *Ultimate Comics Captain America,* and who better to write it than Marvel Architect Jason Aaron — no stranger to tough-guy super heroics after his stints chronicling the all-action adventures of Wolverine, Ghost Rider and the Punisher. Reunited with *Wolverine: Weapon X* collaborator Ron Garney for the high-octane, four-issue series, Jason pits Ultimate Cap against his Vietnam War-era counterpart in a battle to keep the Super-Soldier serum out of enemy hands. *Spotlight* caught up with Jason partway through the series to rap about Ultimate Cap!

SPOTLIGHT: *Ultimate Comics Captain America* marks your debut in the Ultimate Universe. Are you a fan of what has come before, particularly how Mark Millar has developed the character in *The Ultimates* and *Ultimate Avengers*?

JASON: Yeah, I'm a big fan of the Ultimate Universe, going all the way back to the beginning. And Mark's *Ultimates* run is obviously one of the defining super-hero runs of the last several years.

SPOTLIGHT: When we spoke to Mark about Ultimate Cap, he said he "looks like Brad Pitt, but sort of smells like your granddad." What's your take on the character?

JASON: Part Boy Scout. Part grumpy old man. All hero. But with an edge. And with very definite ideas of how the world should work, ideas he doesn't accept will ever be outdated. I also see him as a guy who's still a "man out of time." He missed out on a lot over the years, a lot of important chunks of American history, and he's still catching up on that — or at times stubbornly refusing to catch up. Marvel Universe Cap has pretty much moved past the "man out of time" phase by this point, but Ultimate Cap still grapples with it. Because of that, I think Ultimate Cap can seem a bit more cantankerous and pigheaded. But at the end of the day, they're both still the greatest heroes their world has ever seen.

SPOTLIGHT: You highlight the markedly different role Cap plays in the Ultimate Universe in his scene with Carol Danvers in the second issue, which must have been fun to write.

JASON: Yeah, it was nice to poke a little fun at the idea of "Cap going rogue" being something he seems to do every other Tuesday.

SPOTLIGHT: There's also a nice touch in that story where you play on Ultimate Cap's famous disdain for the French.

JASON: I, personally, have nothing but goodwill for the French. Cap? Not so much.

WRITER JASON AARON.

SPOTLIGHT: Your series pits Steve against Frank Simpson, America's Super-Soldier of the Vietnam era, the Ultimate version of the flag-faced Frank Miller character longtime readers know as Nuke. For those who have yet to check out the book, what's his story in the Ultimate Universe, and in what ways does the stark contrast between Steve and Frank allow you to explore Ultimate Cap's character?

JASON: Frank Simpson started out much like Steve Rogers. He was just a patriotic kid who wanted to do his part for his country. He volunteered to follow in Steve's

Like the cut of Jason Aaron's jib? Want to learn more? Check out the following collected editions and series, and tell your comic shop *Spotlight* sent you!

GHOST RIDER

It's a case of "Ghost Riders in the sky" as blazing-skulled brothers Johnny Blaze and Danny Ketch race to the gates of heaven to stave off an assault by a rogue angel and a veritable antichrist. Gun-toting nuns, a villain with an eyeball for a head and Daimon Hellstrom — an Aaron favorite — round out a high-octane grindhouse epic spanning sixteen issues of *Ghost Rider* and the climactic *Heaven's on Fire* limited series.

Collected editions: Get it *all* in the *Ghost Rider by Jason Aaron Omnibus HC*!

WOLVERINE: WEAPON X

After clicking on the entertaining chase tale "Get Mystique" in the pages of *Wolverine*, Jason and Ron Garney launched this title. Adamantium soldiers! Logan in an insane asylum! A new girlfriend! Two Captain Americas! And a boatload of Deathloks! All capped off with a touching final-issue tribute to the dearly departed Nightcrawler.

Collected editions: See the *Wolverine Weapon X Vol. 1: Adamantium Men*, *Vol. 2: Insane in the Brain* and *Vol. 3: Tomorrow Dies Today* Premiere HCs/TPBs!

PUNISHERMAX

United with renowned *Punisher* artist Steve Dillon, Jason gets twisted in this brutal, adults-only series. Witness the rise of Wilson Fisk, a Kingpin of Crime more ruthless than ever before, and a maniacal take on Bullseye not to be missed! Jason and Steve ratchet up the violence as the blood flows, the bodies pile up and readers beg for more!

Collected editions: See the *PunisherMAX: Bullseye* and *PunisherMAX: Kingpin* Premiere HCs/TPBs!

WOLVERINE

For years, writers have been putting Logan through hell — but only Jason has done it literally. Relaunching *Wolverine* with artist Renato Guedes, Jason sent the Avenging X-Man to the fiery underworld and forced him to claw his way back out. Meanwhile, a demon wearing his flesh targets his loved ones. As Daimon Hellstrom — told you! — pops up to help out up top, it's Puck to the rescue down below!

Collected editions: Start out with the wonderfully violent *Wolverine: Get Mystique TPB* and move on to the aptly named *Wolverine: Wolverine Goes to Hell* Premiere HC/TPB!

footsteps, to become a new sort of Captain America in the years after Steve disappeared. But instead of World War II, Frank Simpson got the moral quagmire of the Vietnam War. And at one point in the midst of that war he just walked off into the jungle, feeling like he'd been lied to and betrayed by his country. He hasn't been seen since, until he pops up in the modern day — apparently helping to spread the Super-Soldier serum among America's enemies, wanting to arm the rest of the world against what he sees as America's imperialism. When Cap and Nuke finally come face-to-face, Nuke feels like he needs to educate Cap on some of the lessons that he missed while he was trapped in ice — the lessons of Vietnam, of Watergate, etc. Cap, as you can imagine, isn't much interested in listening, but instead has some lessons of his own to lay down.

SPOTLIGHT: This isn't the first comic you've written with ties to the Vietnam War. It's clearly a period that interests you and provides fertile ground for storytelling.

JASON: My cousin, Gustav Hasford, was a Vietnam vet and an author. His book, *The Short-Timers*, was the basis for Stanley Kubrick's *Full Metal Jacket*. And my first-ever comic series was a Vietnam War miniseries for Vertigo called *The Other Side*. So yeah, it's a subject that I feel a real connection to, and one I'll likely continue to explore from time to time over the course of my career.

CAP IN BLACK AND WHITE: COVER PENCILS TO *UCA* #1 BY GARNEY. CHECK OUT RON'S CAP SKETCHBOOK ON THE FOLLOWING PAGES!

IT'S NOT YOUR FAULT YOU'RE SO NAÏVE, ROGERS. YOU WERE TRAPPED IN THAT ICE FOR A VERY LONG TIME.

LET'S BEGIN TO CATCH YOU UP ON SOME OF WHAT YOU MISSED, SHALL WE?

THE WORLD ACCORDING TO NUKE: CAP LEARNS HIS LESSON IN JASON AARON'S ULTIMATE CAPTAIN AMERICA. (ART FROM *UCA #3* BY GARNEY.

"(Ultimate Cap has) definite ideas of how the world should work, ideas he doesn't accept will ever be outdated."

SPOTLIGHT: You mention the plot also involves Frank's version of the serum falling into the hands of enemies of the United States as a kind of Super-Soldier arms race develops. As a writer, do you particularly enjoy rooting super heroics in real-world events and politics?

JASON: I think that's a part of what has always made the Ultimates interesting: looking at them as living and breathing WMDs, and figuring how that would play out on an international scale. This story is very much a story about the legacy of the Vietnam War, but it's also a story about today's global climate.

SPOTLIGHT: You obviously get on well with Ron Garney and like to see him draw the shield after writing Bucky Cap into your *Wolverine: Weapon X* run. What makes him such a great artist for Cap?

JASON: Ron's just a great artist no matter what he's drawing. His penchant for action is unparalleled in my opinion, and I still feel like he's doing some of the best work of his career right now. I'm just happy that I've been a part of that and get to keep working with him.

SPOTLIGHT: Finally, imagine Marvel calls offering you *Captain America* or an *Ultimate Cap* ongoing: Which do you choose?

JASON: Either one would be a thrill, quite honestly. But trust me, I've already got enough on my plate as is.

Check out some of the tasty morsels on Jason's overflowing plate each month in the pages of PunisherMAX *and* Wolverine! *And speaking of* Ultimate Cap *artist Ron Garney? Just turn the page, Friends of Old Marvel!* ■

COVER TO *UCA #4* BY GARNEY.

During a Marvel career spanning two decades, Ron Garney has soared the spaceways with the Silver Surfer, gone on a rollicking rampage with the Incredible Hulk, sliced and diced with Wolverine, and put Spider-Man back in black. But to many fans, Ron's kinetic style will forever be associated with one man: the star-spangled Avenger, Captain America. While it took the controversial "Heroes Reborn" experiment and the resulting "Heroes Return," to bring books like *Avengers*, *Iron Man* and *Thor* back to greatness, the ideal combination of Ron and writer Mark Waid had already restored the shine to Cap's shield in 1995. Their well-received run cut short by "Heroes Reborn," Waid and Garney came back to *Captain America* with "Heroes Return" — but the reunion only lasted five issues, as well as six more of the spinoff series *Sentinel of Liberty*. Fans have wondered ever since what might have been had Waid and Garney's run continued uninterrupted. Now, after years in which his natural affinity for drawing Cap has been glimpsed only in guest appearances, Ron has returned to the character — this time with an Ultimate twist. Here, the artist throws open his archives to reveal sketches and pencils that prove no matter which Cap you're talking about, Ron's the man to draw him.

ON CAP: "I enjoy doing action storytelling — and all the way back to the Kirby era, that's what you get when you read a Cap book: a lot of kinetic action. I think that's a strength of my work. I'm also drawn to the character based on what he represents. I like doing iconic characters. I think it appeals to the mythology in me. We gravitate toward characters we can look up to and follow. Captain America is a character like that, as opposed to a character like Deadpool. Deadpool is a cool character, but he's not iconic."

A Captain America Classicist Shares
A Presentation Of His Best

ULTIMATE
SKETCHBOOK: RON
★★★★★★
GARNEY

ON CHOREOGRAPHING CAP: "My style is somewhere between old-school and contemporary. I have a particular way that I see the action moving and the dynamics of the shield. There's a lot of left-to-right movement in my work, and the way you have to pace the action in Cap — when he throws the shield and how he throws it — is very tricky to pull off. You have to time it correctly."

ON BUCKY CAP: "Even though I drew Bucky in *Wolverine: Weapon X*, he's not really Cap to me. He's an homage to Cap. It's not Superman without Clark Kent, it's not Spider-Man without Peter Parker, and it's not Captain America without Steve Rogers. Bucky can move well, but he could be in any other costume. You don't have the same iconography in the artwork. The iconic images I feel more with Steve Rogers."

ON CAP'S COSTUME: "Spider-Man's probably my favorite, but Cap's costume is up there in my top five. I think it's a very handsome design, especially the red and white around the waist, which I think is unique. Scales or no scales, that is the question! The chainmail has been rendered in more detail over the years. Especially with the *Ultimate Cap* stuff, we have to see all the scales. With the older Cap, we used to see just a rendering of it. Back in the '70s, you couldn't afford to sit there and render each scale like you can now."

ON ULTIMATE CAP: "When I first started working on *Ultimate Cap*, it was very odd because of the attitude difference. In the first issue, I think my style of drawing Cap felt weird with Jason's writing. But as the issues went along, I think that fleshed itself out. I felt like I was getting more into the idea of this guy's facial expressions. He talks and fights in a more raw way than the Marvel Universe Cap. In the last issue, you'll see a big difference. There are a couple of things that happen in that fight scene that would be pretty uncharacteristic for the Marvel Universe Steve Rogers."

ON NUKE: "I thought it was a great choice to use him. It's fun creating some lore for a character from such a legendary run as Frank Miller's 'Born Again.' Visually, all he's got is that tattoo on his face and military fatigues, and that's what makes it work. He doesn't need any more than that. I started out by drawing the tattoo in, and it took a few emails back and forth with the colorist, Jason Keith, to get it to look right. At first, it looked like a plastic sticker on his face. But once we got it to look right, I would basically put the outline of the rectangle on there and leave it up to Jason to color."

ON ULTIMATE CAP'S COSTUME: "Drawing the Ultimate Cap costume made it more fun than rehashing the same old stuff I'd done fifteen years ago. The extra detail in the costume and its more military flavor felt a little more real to me. Having drawn Ultimate Cap and the 616 Cap, I enjoy drawing him without the wings. When you put the wings on him, he becomes the 616 Cap. It's not that you can't take him seriously with the wings, but he becomes less of a bastard than the Ultimate Cap when he has them. They make him a bit lighter. It's easier to take Ultimate Cap seriously. You're more likely to see a guy like Cap one day than Thor, so I think this costume lends itself to that believability. This guy could really exist."